F & P. I

NATURE DETECTIVES

A Walk in the Park

Jo Waters

Chicago, Illinois

Customer Service   888–454–2279

Visit our website at www.heinemannlibrary.com

Photo research by Maria Joannou and Rebecca Sodergren
Designed by Jo Hinton-Malivoire and Tinstar Design Ltd (www.tinstar.co.uk)
Printed and bound in China by South China Printing Company
10 09 08 07 06
10 9 8 7 6 5 4 3 2 1

Library of Congress Cataloging-in-Publication Data
Waters, Jo.
  A walk in the park / Jo Waters.
      p. cm. -- (Nature detectives)
  Includes index.
  ISBN 1-4109-2291-X (library binding-hardcover) -- ISBN 1-4109-2296-0 (pbk.)
  1. Parks--Juvenile literature. 2. Plants--Juvenile literature. 3. Animals--Juvenile literature. I. Title.
  SB481.3.W38 2006
  333.78'3--dc22
                                        2005029318

Acknowledgments
The Publishers would like to thank the following for permission to reproduce photographs:
Alamy Images p. 5; Alamy Images/Anthony Collins p. 20; Corbis pp. 15, 21; Corbis/Jacqui Hurst p.11;
Corbis/Ralph A Clevenger p. 8; Corbis/Phil Schermeister p. 16; FLPA p. 9; FLPA/Jurgen & Christine
Sohns p. 13; Harcourt Education Ltd/Malcolm Harris pp. 4, 6, 14, 17, 23; Getty Images/Botanica p.7;
Getty Images /Photographers Choice p. 10; Masterfile/Matt Brasier p. 22; Photolibrary.com/Oxford
Scientific Films pp. 12, 18, 19.

Cover photograph reproduced with permission of Getty Images.

Our thanks to Annie Davy and Michael Scott for their assistance in the preparation of this book.

Some words are shown in bold, **like this**. You can find out
what they mean by looking in the glossary.

Contents

At the Park

Where are we?
We are at the park!

Lots of people have fun here.

Fabulous Flowers

Look at the flowers.
Can you see the **petals**?

petals

Busy bees buzz around
the flowers.

7

Another Visitor

Who else is visiting the flowers?

A colorful butterfly!

9

Grass

Each **blade** of grass is a leaf.

10

Down in the grass
little snails are hiding.

11

Spotty Minibeast

Who is climbing up the stalk?
A ladybug!

Ladybugs have lots of spots.
How many can you see?

13

Wiggly Worm

Worms live in the earth.
They wiggle and crawl.

Tall Trees

Look at the shapes of the leaves.

Have you ever felt a tree's **bark**?
Is it rough or smooth?

Who is Hiding?

Sitting in the tree ...
a squirrel!

What could he be eating?

On the Pond

A duck and her ducklings go for a swim. Quack quack!

Look closer. A duck's feather is made of lots of tiny hairs.

Good-bye Park

The sun is going down.
It is getting chilly. Brrr.

22

Smell one last flower.
It is time to go home.

23

Glossary

bark outside covering of a tree
blade leaf of grass
petal part of a flower that is
usually colored

Index

Notes for adults

Exploring the natural world at an early age can help promote awareness of the environment and general understanding of life processes. Discussing the seasons with children can be a good way of helping them understand the concepts of time, patterns, and change. Identifying features that people share with insects and animals can promote understanding of similarities.

Follow-up activities
- Encourage children to think and talk about why people should take care of the environment and not damage plants or harm animals.
- Encourage children to use all their senses to feel, look at, and describe a leaf. Invite comments about all aspects of leaves, including color, texture, smell, and sound.
- The children could make a collage or leaf prints as part of an art session.